Other books by Robin Conrad Sturm:

Breathing Life Into Dance –One Teacher's Perspective (second revised edition)

Hannah Finds Her Voice

Daniel Doesn't Dance

Finally Friends

by Robin Conrad Sturm

Illustrations by Laurie Mang

Finally Friends

For all other questions, contact the publisher at rob2stu@aol.com.

Robin Conrad Sturm — First Edition

ISBN 978-1-935355-24-3

Printed in the United States of America

This story is dedicated to all of my dancer friends of my youth –

We sure learned a lot, didn't we?

I would like to thank all of my students, past, present, and future, who have learned the strength of tirelessly pursuing their dreams, and finding out that the struggle is always worth it.

Two ladies in a coffee shop sat chatting; they were friends.
They danced together years ago when their careers began.

Although they seemed so happy now, this wasn't always true-
A dangerous plague once sneaked into the world they both clung to.

Madeline and a friend named Meg danced since they were quite young.
Their lives revolved around ballet, on dance their dreams had hung.

It wasn't just their dancing that made their faces glow; their friendly smiles and once humble hearts made others love them so.

The younger students tried to be like dancers they admired-

So these two ladies topped the list; the others were inspired!

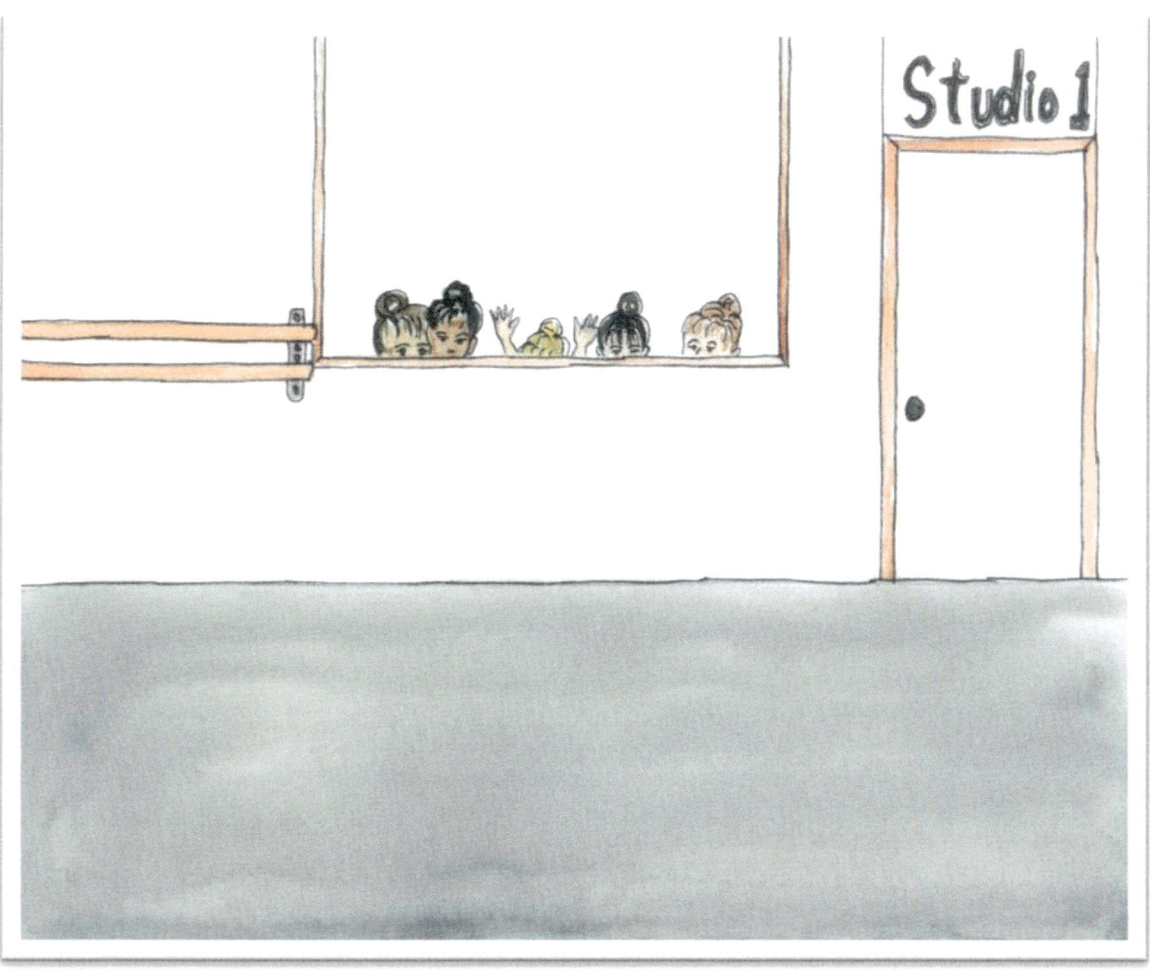

They always worked for better parts, they practiced everyday.
Their efforts were rewarded when they heard the director say,

"Meg and Madeline, I'm proud of progress you have made!
I'd love for both of you to learn the solo in my ballet!"

Meg and Madeline presumed that they were going to be the very best that the director ever wanted to see.

Believing the part was theirs to have, they knew they'd alternate for first and second cast on different nights. Fame was their fate!

So work they did, and it paid off, but they felt they alone should get the solos and the leads that no one else should own.

At first they didn't know which one was first to get the chance to do the role they both had learned. Who would be first to dance?

It would be weeks until they knew the first to get the part, but they kept working, unaware that others could share their art!

But many dancers training hard had come into their own, and Meg and Madeline forgot they didn't dance alone.

Another dancer, Lydia, had caught the director's eye. She was so beautiful to watch but was so very shy.

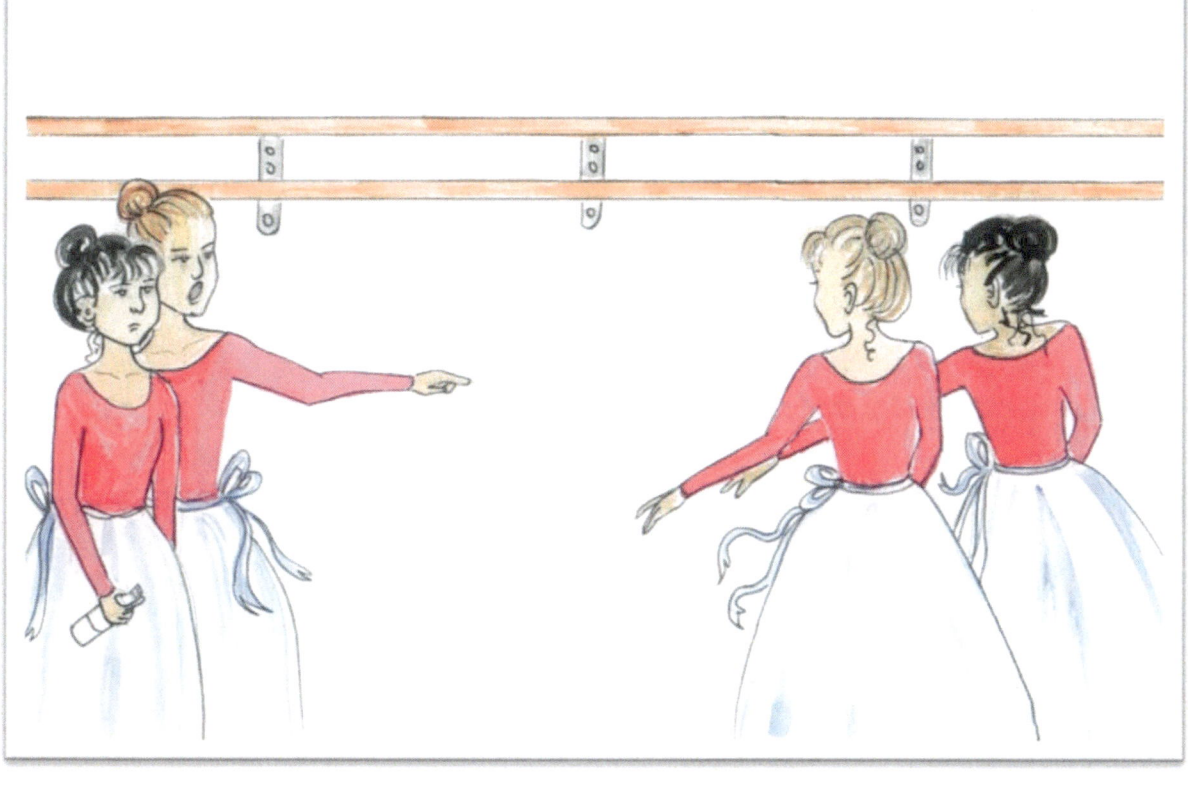

And she was not the only one who moved up through the ranks.
As others came, the ballet grew, and all deserved a chance.

Now Meg and Madeline believed they were the only ones who should have solos on the stage - the others should be gone!

And so that dangerous plague with many cousins
settled in: gossip, envy, pride took hold -
and whispering began.

Meg and Madeline would glare at others taking part.
They'd point, and scowl, and say mean things of others
working hard!

In anger they would mock the teacher in the dressing room.
The other dancers heard while Meg and Madeline spread their gloom.

Their angry gossip spread like a disease to everyone, so students who looked up to them began to think it fun.

And even those who disagreed were too afraid
to say –
They just kept quiet, staying silent as they went about
their day.

See, sometimes being mean can seem like fun to those
who fear their own ability's at risk, or even their career!

This dangerous disease affects all those who give it ear, especially when their target "accidentally" overhears.

Though Lydia knew the unkind words about her spread so fast, she never stopped being kind and worked her best at every task.

Lydia was a gentle soul, her kindness was well known. Her shyness was perceived as soft, but her will was strong as stone.

But Lydia couldn't let the unkind words fall off her heart.
She'd think about them day and night - the arrows had found their mark.

She danced her hardest everyday despite words that were said.
And those who truly knew her best just let mean words fall dead.

Lydia's dancing flourished more each day, and others noticed, too.
And then one day the director said, "I've got a solo for you!"

Lydia was elated! All knew how hard she'd worked to do her very best, but now...real trouble began to lurk!

Meg and Madeline found out that Lydia had received the solo *they* assumed they had; they felt they'd been deceived!

They passed around the story that Lydia's mom and dad had bribed the director for Lydia's roles they felt *they* should have had!

Although she knew she earned her part, poor Lydia went home and cried –
Her heart was breaking; she was afraid friends would believe those lies.

Meg and Madeline never knew ballet was meant to be the art where *all* onstage were lovely dancers to be seen.

The words they said pierced Lydia's heart; they were extremely cruel.
"Her turns are bad, her leg's too low, she should've quit ballet school!"

They told the other dancers that Lydia's dancing was too boring –
"When I watch Lydia dance I always hear the audience snoring!"

But Lydia just kept pushing through; she'd help those who were younger.
She understood that *many* good dancers make a ballet stronger!

By staying humble, kind, and having devotion to her art, her character shone through her eyes; her dance expressed her heart.

But Meg and Madeline had trouble understanding this.
They let their pride and jealousy deprive them of their
bliss.

The bitter words and angry thoughts eventually
slipped away,
And Meg decided ballet wasn't where she wanted to
stay.

She chose a path more suited for her talents, so she
left.
And that meant Madeline was all alone –she was
bereft!

Ballet directors never prefer to have only one –
When *many* dancers grace the stage, it makes it much
more fun!

When dancers come together with their talents at one
time,
the art that is expressed is not just gorgeous, it's
sublime!

Everyone else soon wearied of the poison those two spread;
they set their sights on doing their best, they wanted joy instead!

They found that dancing towards a goal united as a team
made everyone come out on top, fulfilling *all* their dreams!

When Meg had left, our Lydia saw that Madeline was so sad –
Apparently she felt Meg was the only friend she had.

Sweet Lydia just couldn't let poor Madeline disappear; she saw that Madeline's talent could become a great career.

So Lydia held her breath, then asked sad Madeline to be her friend.
She knew that nothing else could change till someone tried to bend.

It didn't happen right away, the hurts caused icy silence.
But gradually both dancers learned respect for each other's talents.

Then after a while, all dancing aside, they finally could discover
their likes and dislikes and humor made them actually like each other!

And Madeline soon found out that when one dancer gets a part,
it doesn't mean that no one else can exercise their art.

She found that working as a team, each one can do their best;
when working together creating dreams, the true art is expressed!

So now the years have passed and two old friends can sit and chat
while sipping coffee, sharing jokes, and talk of this and that.

They finally learned the joy of sharing what they both held dear.
For they saw what they had almost lost before it disappeared.

Who knew that Madeline and Lydia could be the best of friends?
They're in each other's hearts for good, their memories will never end!

Their friendship now is precious and will never, ever fade.
They learned to share their dreams, their art -
And a special bond was made.

The End

About the Author:

Robin Conrad Sturm began her ballet training at seven and a half years of age with Mary Day, and went on to become a graduate of the Academy of the Washington School of the Ballet. She was a full-scholarship student at the American Ballet Theatre School and the School of American Ballet in New York. She was a founding member of the Washington Ballet. Ms. Sturm and her husband, Bob, have three grown children, Jeremy, Rebekah, and Samantha. They live in Manassas, Virginia, where they co-direct the Asaph Dance Ensemble.

Made in the USA
Columbia, SC
14 May 2017